Math
in Space

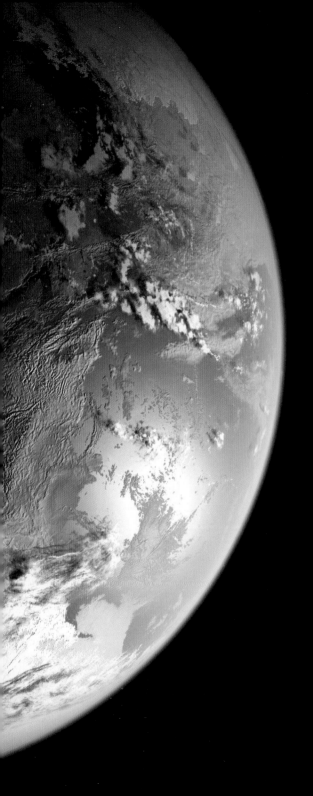

Thanks to the creative team:
Senior Editor: Alice Peebles
Illustration: Dan Newman
Fact checking: Tom Jackson
Picture Research: Nic Dean
Design: Perfect Bound Ltd

Hungry Tomato®
A division of Lerner Publishing Group, Inc.
241 First Avenue North
Minneapolis, MN 55401 USA

For reading levels and more information,
look up this title at www.lernerbooks.com.

Main body text set in Panton Regular 10.5/13.

Library of Congress Cataloging-in-Publication Data

Names: Dickmann, Nancy, author.
Title: Math in space / Nancy Dickmann.
Description: Minneapolis : Hungry Tomato, [2018] | Series:
The amazing world of math | Audience: Ages 8–12. | Audience:
Grades 4 to 6.
Identifiers: LCCN 2017060519 (print) | LCCN 2017056679
(ebook) | ISBN 9781541523920 (eb pdf) | ISBN 9781541501003
(lb : alk. paper)
Subjects: LCSH: Mathematics—Juvenile literature. | Space
sciences—Mathematics—Juvenile literature.
Classification: LCC QA135.6 (print) | LCC QA135.6 .D545 2018
(ebook) | DDC 520.1/51—dc23

LC record available at https://lccn.loc.gov/2017060519

Manufactured in the United States of America
1-43771-33629-2/5/2018

The Amazing World of Math

Math
in Space

Nancy Dickmann

HUNGRY TOMATO®

Minneapolis

View of Earth from the
surface of the moon.

Contents

Math
All around Us

*If you think that math is just a subject at school, think again! Numbers, shapes, and **temperature** all play a role in shaping the universe around us.*

Math Is Out There...

Did you know that there are patterns in crystals and giant swirling **galaxies**? Or that a numerical coincidence is the cause of amazing solar **eclipses**? The universe is huge and incredibly complex, but it still follows rules—and many of these rules are based on math. In fact, some things are either too small or too far away to see clearly, so we rely on math to work out what's out there.

*There is even math behind a solar eclipse! The **moon**'s size, shape, and distance from Earth enable it to block the sun perfectly (see pages 14–15).*

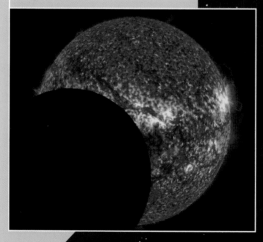

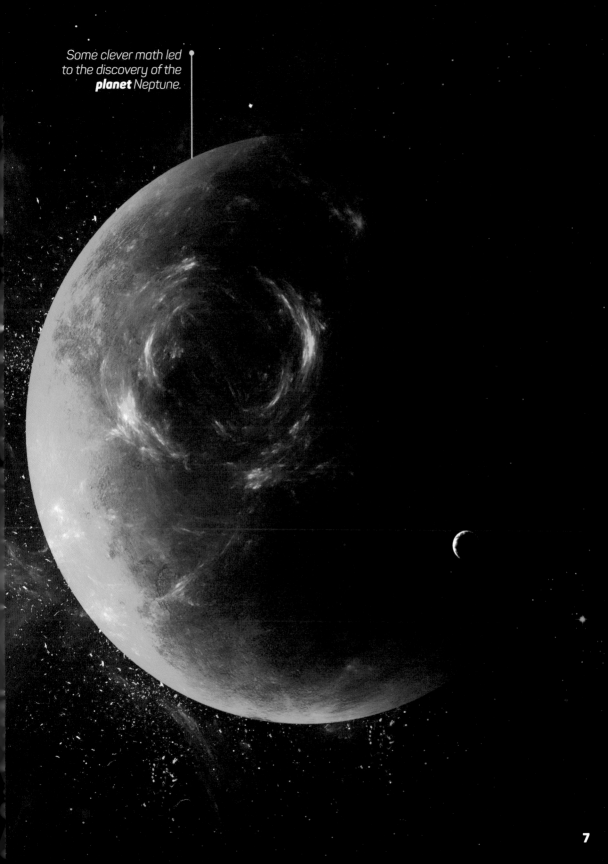

Some clever math led to the discovery of the **planet** Neptune.

A World of Spheres

Earth is spherical, or ball-shaped. So are the moon and sun—and the rest of the planets too. In fact, most space objects over a certain size are spherical. But why?

Gravity

Gravity is the force that attracts objects to each other. The more **mass** an object has, the stronger its gravity. With a large object like a planet, gravity pulls equally on all sides, pulling everything in towards the center. This results in a sphere shape. No matter whether a planet is made of gas or rock, its gravity has the same effect.

Smaller objects, like **comets** and **asteroids**, are also held together by gravity. However, they have much less mass, so their gravity is weaker. It is not strong enough to pull them into perfect spherical shapes.

The asteroid Ida (seen with its tiny moon Dactyl from the Galileo spacecraft) is only about 19 miles (11 km) wide—far too small to be spherical.

The moon is small compared to Earth, but it is still big enough to be spherical.

Not Quite Perfect

Most spherical space objects **rotate**, or spin, around a central **axis**. The axis is an imaginary line through the center of a sphere. With some large objects, the speed of rotation makes them bulge out around the middle. They are no longer perfect spheres but look more like a basketball that someone has sat on, squashing it slightly.

Jupiter spins very fast, and its equator bulges out quite a bit.

Math in Action!

From Earth, the moon looks like a circle. We find any circle's **circumference** with a special number called pi (written as π)—roughly 3.14. Take the circle's **radius** (the distance from the center to the edge), multiply by 2, then by π. Use a calculator to find the circumference of an asteroid with a radius of 100 miles.

Symmetry in Space

Spheres are symmetrical—if you split one in half, both halves will be identical. Many galaxies are symmetrical too but in a different way.

Giant Galaxies

Galaxies are enormous groups of stars, containing billions of individual stars. Galaxies are held together by—you guessed it—gravity. Most galaxies are roughly shaped like flat discs. They often have long arms that form a spiral shape as the entire galaxy rotates.

M81 is a spiral galaxy that shows rotational symmetry.

The photo of M81 has been rotated 180°. The shape of the galaxy still looks the same.

Spinning Around

An object that forms a mirror image of itself is just one type of symmetry. Spiral galaxies do not have this. Drawing a line through the middle would give you two halves that look fairly similar but are not mirror images. Instead, some spiral galaxies have a different type of symmetry, called rotational symmetry.

If you take an object with rotational symmetry and rotate it by a partial turn, it will look identical. Some objects repeat after a one-quarter or one-third turn. Spiral galaxies usually repeat after a one-half turn of 180 **degrees** (written as 180°).

Math in Action!

Try designing a spaceship or alien life form that has rotational symmetry. Once you've finished, lay a sheet of tracing paper over your drawing and trace its outline. Rotate the tracing paper slowly, watching to see if the two pictures match up. If they do, your drawing has rotational symmetry.

This symbol has rotational symmetry. Turning it by one-third of a complete circle will give you an identical shape.

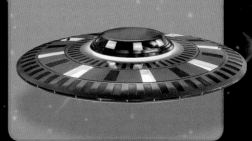

The Moon's Changing Shape

Sometimes the moon appears round, and sometimes it is a thin crescent. But the moon is a sphere, so how can it appear to change shape?

Lit by the Sun

The moon does not produce its own light. Instead, it reflects light from the sun. At any given time, only half the moon—the half facing the sun—is bright. The half that is facing away from the sun is in darkness.

Every month, the moon makes one complete circuit around the Earth. Depending on where it is in its journey, we see different amounts of the lit half. When the Earth, moon, and sun are in a straight line, with the moon and sun on opposite sides of the Earth, we see the entire lit face of the moon. This is a full moon.

We can often see the moon and its changing shape during the day.

A thin crescent moon can be a dramatic sight.

All about Angles

The Earth, sun, and moon form an **angle**, with Earth at the **vertex**, or point. An angle is a measure of a turn, and there are 360° in a full turn. When the Earth, moon, and sun form an angle of 90° (a quarter turn), we see half of the moon's lit side and half of the dark side. This makes the moon look like a half-circle from Earth.

This diagram shows eight phases of the moon as seen from Earth. The dotted lines represent your line of sight during these phases. The larger moons at each point show what you would see during that phase.

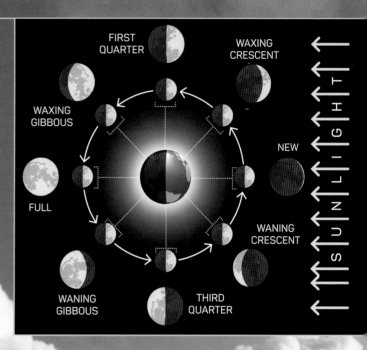

FIRST QUARTER

WAXING CRESCENT

WAXING GIBBOUS

NEW

FULL

WANING CRESCENT

WANING GIBBOUS

THIRD QUARTER

SUNLIGHT

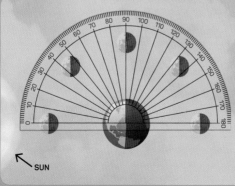

SUN

Math in Action!

Use a **protractor** to measure the angles formed by the Earth, the sun, and the moon in this diagram. Line up the protractor so the midpoint is over the center of the Earth. The 0 line should align with the sunlight at left. What number falls on the moon during the waxing **gibbous** phase?

13

Eclipse!

Solar eclipses are rare but dramatic. They happen when the moon slowly moves in front of the sun, causing a drop in temperature and eerie darkness in the middle of the day.

SUN
*Diameter 864,600 miles (1,391,000 km)
Distance from Earth 92,900,000 miles
(149,600,000 km)*

When the Earth moves between the moon and the sun, it causes a lunar eclipse.

Blocked Out

For a total solar eclipse to occur, the Earth, the moon, and the sun have to line up perfectly. As the moon passes between the Earth and the sun, it blocks the sun's light. This creates a shadow that falls on Earth. If you are lucky enough to be in the area of shadow, you will see the sun disappear for a few minutes.

Big but Far Away

Perfect solar eclipses are down to a lucky coincidence. The sun's **diameter** is about 400 times the diameter of the moon. If the two objects were the same distance from the Earth, the sun would appear to be 400 times bigger than the moon.

Luckily for us, the sun is much farther away! And the farther away an object is, the smaller it looks. The sun is about 400 times farther away from Earth than the moon is. So the two objects appear more or less the same size in the sky—making the moon the perfect size to cause an eclipse. No other planet in our solar system has a moon exactly the right size, so only Earth has perfect solar eclipses.

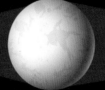

MOON
Diameter 3,476 km
Distance from Earth 384,400 km

Total eclipse

Partial eclipse

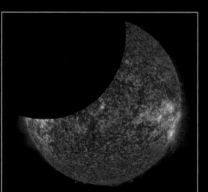

At the beginning of a solar eclipse, the moon appears to take a bite out of the sun.

Math in Action!

Jupiter's moon Ganymede is about 3,270 miles (5,300 km) in diameter. The diameter of the sun is about 864,600 miles (1,400,000 km). How many times bigger is the sun? Use a calculator to work out the answer.

Finding Planets with Math

Some space objects are discovered with a telescope. Others—like the planet Neptune—were discovered using math!

Jupiter

Venus

Mars

Mercury

Earth

Asteroid belt

Saturn

[Planets' distance from the svun not to scale]

Mystery Planet

In 1781, the planet Uranus was discovered with a telescope. **Astronomers** tracked the new planet's path and found that its **orbit** wasn't quite as expected. The gravity of another large object must be disturbing its orbit.

Mathematicians started doing the math to locate this object, and in 1846 Urbain Le Verrier announced his results. An astronomer then used his powerful telescope to search the sky where Le Verrier predicted the new planet would be. He found Neptune within an hour.

Urbain Le Verrier's prediction of Neptune made him famous.

Getting It Wrong

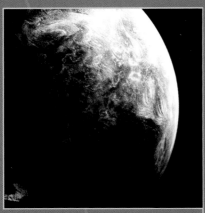

An earlier astronomer called Johann Bode had also tried to use math to predict planets. The gaps between the planets seemed to follow a mathematical **pattern**. When Uranus was discovered, it fit the pattern too. Was Bode on to something?

According to Bode's Law, there should have been another planet between Mars and Jupiter, and the asteroid belt was soon discovered to fill this gap. However, Neptune didn't fit the pattern at all. Astronomers now believe that Bode's Law is just a coincidence.

Neptune was named after the Roman god of the sea.

Uranus

Neptune

The farther away from the Sun that planets are, the bigger are the gaps between them.

Math in Action!

Follow the instructions to fill in the table and see how Bode worked out his predicted distances. The final numbers are **astronomical units** (AU).

	Mercury	Venus	Earth	Mars	Asteroids	Jupiter	Saturn	Uranus	Neptune
Double the number to the left	0	3	6	12	24	48	96		
Add 4 to the number above	4	7	10	16	28	52	100		
Divide the number above by 10	0.4	0.7	1.0	1.6	2.8	5.2	10.0		

To find Neptune's distance from the sun, you would then multiply the number in the yellow box by the Earth's distance from the sun. That is, if Bode's Law actually worked—which it doesn't!

Water, Ice, or Gas?

*Stars are made of gas, Mercury is **solid,** and the Earth's oceans are liquid. These different forms are all caused by temperature.*

Temperature and State

Scientists measure temperature on the Celsius scale, which starts at −273 (−459.4°F), the coldest possible temperature. Nearly every substance would be solid at −273°C (−459.4°F). But each substance has a **melting point**: a temperature at which it turns from a solid to a liquid. Then comes the boiling point, at which it turns from a liquid to a gas.

The melting point of water is 0 °C (32°F) and its **boiling point** is 100°C (212°F). The gases in our air have much lower boiling points. For example, the boiling point of nitrogen is −196°C (−320.8°F). That's how cold it would have to be on Earth for the nitrogen gas in the atmosphere to turn into a liquid.

The inside of Jupiter's moon Europa (below) is warm enough to create an ocean of liquid water. Its surface temperature is very cold, freezing the top layer of the ocean into an icy crust.

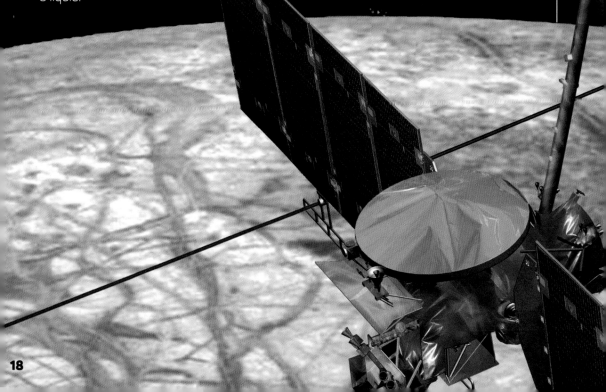

These blue areas on Titan's surface are lakes of methane.

Liquid World

Saturn's moon Titan is the only moon in the solar system with liquid on its surface. But Titan is so cold that any water would be frozen solid. Instead, Titan's lakes are filled with methane. On Earth, methane is a gas, but Titan's low temperature keeps it in its liquid form.

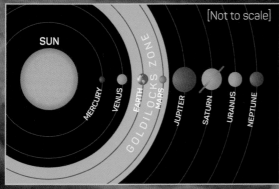

[Not to scale]

SUN

GOLDILOCKS ZONE

MERCURY VENUS EARTH MARS JUPITER SATURN URANUS NEPTUNE

*Planets in the **Goldilocks Zone** of a solar system are not too hot or too cold, but just right for water in its liquid form, a necessity for life to exist. A faraway planet called Kepler-186f is the right distance from its star to have liquid water.*

Math in Action!

The melting point of gold is 1,063°C (1,945.4°F). Its boiling point is 2,966°C (5,370.8°F). What is the difference between these two numbers? (Use a calculator if you need to.)

The Incredible Shrinking Comet

Every 76 years, Halley's Comet passes close to Earth. And each time it returns, it's a little bit smaller than it was before . . .

Icy Visitors

Comets are lumps of rock, dust, ice, and frozen gases. Most are only a few miles across. Every so often, they travel on a long, looping path that circles around the sun, then takes them back where they came from.

Feeling the Heat

As a comet gets close to the sun, it starts to warm up. Its frozen gases boil to return to their gaseous state. This creates an atmosphere (called a coma) around the the body of the comet. A type of wind that comes from the sun blows on the comet. It pushes the gas and dust of the coma out into a long tail.

The comet leaves behind the gas and dust in its tail as it hurtles through space. With each pass around the sun, it only loses a small percentage of its mass. For example, Halley's Comet is about 9 miles (15 km) across. With each trip, it sheds a layer of rock and ice about 18 feet (5.5 m) deep. After many, many more trips around the sun, there will be so little left that it will disintegrate completely.

A comet's tail can stretch out for millions of kilometres.

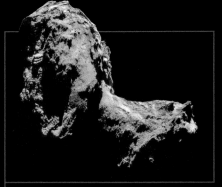

In 2014, the Rosetta spacecraft went into orbit around a comet called 67P, taking photos of its icy body.

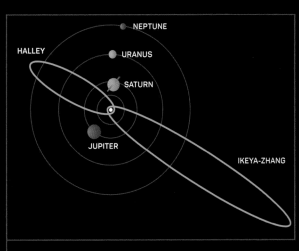

NEPTUNE
HALLEY
URANUS
SATURN
JUPITER
IKEYA-ZHANG

A planet's orbit is nearly round, but comets travel in much longer, narrower loops.

Math in Action!

A comet has a mass of about 11,000,000,000 (11 billion) tons. Imagine that it lost 1% of its mass on a trip around the sun. What would its new mass be?

Cool Crystals

What do a diamond and a pencil have in common? The answer might surprise you . . .

Quartz is made of silicon and oxygen atoms joined together in a crystal structure.

It's Elemental!

Everything in the universe is made up of the same basic **elements**. There are nearly 100 elements that occur naturally, including iron, gold, and oxygen. Elements can be found on their own, or combined with other elements. Most things—like planets, plastics, plants, and humans—are made up of a mixture of different elements.

The tiniest unit of an element is an **atom**. These particles are much too small to see. In a solid, the atoms are tightly packed together. The atoms often form a regular pattern of repeated shapes. With some elements, such as carbon, the atoms can arrange themselves in more than one pattern.

Different Forms

The "lead" in a pencil is actually graphite, which is a form of the element carbon. In graphite, the carbon atoms are arranged in rows of six-sided hexagons. Each atom is attached to three other atoms. They form flat sheets that slide easily over each other.

Graphite's layer structure makes it slippery and not very hard.

Diamonds are also made of pure carbon, but their atoms are arranged differently. They form a structure called a crystal. Each atom is attached to four other atoms, not three, and there are no separate layers.

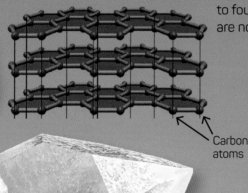

Carbon atoms

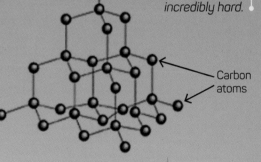

A diamond's crystal structure makes it incredibly hard.

Carbon atoms

Math in Action!

Look at the diagram and try making a model of a diamond with toothpicks and marshmallows or candies. The are the atoms, and the toothpicks are the connections between each atom. Remember: each atom must be connected to four other atoms.

Spirals in Space

Shapes are everywhere in nature, from spherical planets to cone-shaped mountains. But one very special shape has become linked to enormous galaxies: the spiral.

Types of Spiral

In mathematical terms, a spiral is a curve that winds around and around a central point. As the curve gets longer, it moves farther and farther from the central point. There are different types of spiral. In some, the distance from the center point increases quickly. In others, it increases more slowly. Many galaxies are shaped like a type of spiral called a logarithmic spiral.

Tracing the arms of a galaxy shows the spiral shape.

How Galaxies Form

Galaxies come in different shapes, but spirals are the most common. Astronomers believe that in the early universe, spirals didn't exist. Galaxies back then were clumpy and irregular. Over billions of years, the clumps in many galaxies stretched out into spiral arms. The first spiral galaxies appeared when the universe was about 3.6 billion years old.

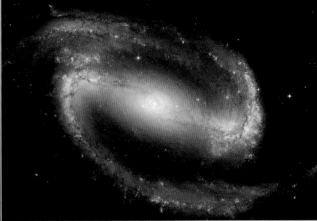

Living creatures like the nautilus make shells that have a spiral shape similar to the shape of galaxies.

Some spiral galaxies have a group of stars shaped like a flat bar across the center. They are called barred spirals.

Math in Action!

Astronomers believe that our galaxy, the Milky Way, has four main arms forming its spiral. Two of the arms have a lot of stars, and two of them have fewer stars. If the more densely packed arms each have 65 billion stars, and the lighter arms each have 35 billion, how many stars would there be in total? (No one actually knows exactly how many stars there are in the Milky Way!)

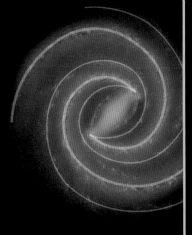

What's Out There?

Humans have long wondered if alien life exists.
But how likely is it? It's a question of **probability**.

What Is Probability?

Probability is a mathematical way of stating
how likely it is that some event will occur.
For example, a weather forecast might say
that there is a 20% chance of rain. Or if you
are throwing a die, it will land with one of its
six sides facing up—so the probability of it
landing on the number 5 is 1 in 6.

There are billions
of galaxies in the
universe, each
containing billions
of stars.

The universe is so huge
that even if alien life does
exist, we may never find it.

A planet orbiting a star other than the sun is called an exoplanet. We have found thousands so far, but there are probably many more.

The Drake Equation

In 1960, an astronomer called Frank Drake tried to work out an equation that would show the probability of intelligent life existing elsewhere in our galaxy. It was based on things like the number of stars, the percentage of stars that have planets and the percentage of planets that have the right conditions for life.

The problem was, Drake couldn't attach accurate numbers to his equation. He simply didn't know, for example, the average number of planets per star in the Milky Way. And we still don't! We are learning a lot about exoplanets, but it will be a long time before we can fill in the blanks in Drake's equation.

Math in Action!

Imagine a galaxy of 200 stars, where 50% of the stars have planets around them. For the stars that have planets, the average number of planets per star is 4. How many planets are there in the galaxy?

Math in Action:
Answers & Tips

How did you do with the 10 math challenges? Here are the correct answers and some tips on how to work them out.

Page 9: The circumference of an asteroid with a radius of 100 miles is 628 miles. To work this out, you start by multiplying the radius by 2: 100 x 2 = 200. Now you need to multiply 200 by pi, which is roughly 3.14. This gives you 200 x 3.14 = 628.

If you want to work it out without a calculator, use place value to help you. You know that 200 = 2 x 100, so you can make the problem easier by working out 2 x 3.14 = 6.28. Now, to multiply this by 100, just move the decimal point two places to the right and you get 628.

Page 11: Did your drawing match up with the tracing paper when you rotated it? If not, try designing another spaceship or alien. It might help to think about things in nature that have rotational symmetry. For example, starfish and jellyfish do, and so do many flowers.

Page 13: During the waxing gibbous phase, the angle measures 135°. At the first quarter, the angle is 90°, and at the full moon it is 180° (which is a straight line). The waxing gibbous phase falls exactly halfway between these two. The difference between 90 and 180 is 90, and half of that is 45. So the waxing gibbous angle must be another 45° past 90°: 90 + 45 = 135.

Page 15: The diameter of the sun is about 264 times bigger than the diameter of Ganymede. This is a tricky division problem, so use a calculator:
864,600 ÷ 3,270 = 264 (rounded down to the nearest whole number).

So the Sun is 264 times wider than Ganymede, but it is 728 times farther from Jupiter than Ganymede is. If you were on Jupiter, Ganymede would look much bigger than the Sun. It can completely block out the Sun, creating a solar eclipse, but as it looks so much bigger, the effect wouldn't be as breathtaking as on Earth.

Page 17: The number in the yellow box is 38.8. The completed table is below.

	Mercury	Venus	Earth	Mars	Asteroids	Jupiter	Saturn	Uranus	Neptune
Double the number to the left	0	3	6	12	24	48	96	192	384
Add 4 to the number above	4	7	10	16	28	52	100	196	388
Divide the number above by 10	0.4	0.7	1.0	1.6	2.8	5.2	10.0	19.6	38.8

Page 19: The difference between the melting and boiling point of gold is 1,903°C. This is a simple subtraction problem: 2966 − 1063 = 1903.

Page 21: The comet's new mass is 10,890,000,000 tons. To work this out, first you need to find how much mass it loses. It loses 1% of its mass, which is the same as $1/100$. To divide 11,000,000,000 by 100, just knock off two zeroes. The result is 110,000,000 tons of mass lost.

Now you need to subtract 110,000,000 from the comet's original mass of 11,000,000,000. These are big numbers, but you can work it out using column subtraction:

$$\begin{array}{r} 11,000,000,000 \\ -\ 110,000,000 \\ \hline 10,890,000,000 \end{array}$$

Page 23: Does your diamond model look like the diagram? If you're having trouble, a good way to start is by making a bunch of tetragonal shapes. These are made from a piece of candy with four toothpicks sticking out. If you set one of these shapes on a table, three of the toothpicks will form legs, spread out in a triangle shape. The fourth toothpick will point straight up.

Once you have several of these tetragonal shapes, you can start sticking them together. Attach a sweet to each of the three legs of the first shape, then attach another shape hanging down from each of the new sweets. Keep adding sweets and tetragonal shapes until you have a large diamond molecule!

Page 25: This version of the Milky Way has 200 billion stars. You need to add 65 billion + 65 billion + 35 billion + 35 billion. To make it easier, forget about the billions for now and just work out 65 + 65 + 35 + 35. It might be easier to add up 60 + 60 + 30 + 30 to get 180. Then you add 5 + 5 + 5 + 5 to get 20. Now add the two together: 180 + 20 = 200. Don't forget to turn it back into billions for a final answer of 200 billion stars.

Page 27: There are 400 planets in the galaxy. To work this out, first you need to find the number of stars with planets around them. There are 200 stars, and 50% have planets. 50% is equal to $50/100$ or ½. Half of 200 is 100.

The average number of planets per star is 4, so you need to multiply this by the number of planets with stars: 100 x 4 = 400.

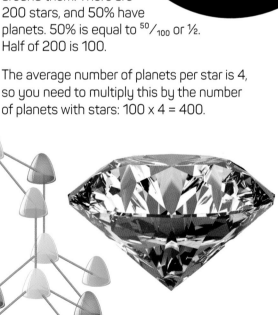

Glossary

angle: the space between two lines that come from a central point. Angles are measured in degrees.

asteroid: a large chunk of rock left over from when the planets formed

astronomer: person who studies the sun, planets, and other objects in space

astronomical unit (AU): unit of measure based on the distance from Earth to the sun, which is roughly 93,000,000 miles (150,000,000 km)

atom: the smallest unit of a substance, which cannot be broken down into different substances

axis: an imaginary line through the middle of a planet or moon, around which it spins

boiling point: the temperature at which a liquid turns into a gas

circumference: the length of the line that forms the outside edge of a circle

comet: rocky, icy object that travels in a long, looping path around the sun

degree: unit for measuring angles, written as °

diameter: the width of a circle, which passes through the circle's center

eclipse: one object in space being temporarily blocked out by another

element: a substance that cannot be broken down or separated into other substances

galaxy: collection of billions of stars held together by gravity

gibbous: phase of the moon when more than half of it, but less than the full circle is lit up

Goldilocks Zone: the region around a star at the right distance for liquid water to exist on the surface of planets

gravity: a force that attracts all objects to each other. Gravity is the force that makes objects fall to the ground

mass: the total amount of matter in an object or space

melting point: the temperature at which a solid turns into a liquid

moon: object that orbits a planet or asteroid

orbit: the path that an object takes around a larger object; or, to take such a path

pattern: an arrangement of shapes, lines or numbers that can be repeated over and over

planet: large, spherical object that orbits the sun or another star

probability: a number that expresses how likely something is to happen

protractor: a semi-circular instrument used to measure angles

radius: the distance from the center of a circle or sphere to its edge

rotate: to spin around a central axis

solid: having a firm shape that can be measured in length, width, and height

temperature: how hot or cold something is

vertex: the point at which two lines or faces meet to form an angle

Amazing Math Facts

Between the orbits of Mars and Jupiter is a huge ring of smaller objects called asteroids. This is the asteroid belt. Some asteroids are only the size of a car, but a few are big enough for their gravity to make them spherical. The biggest object in the asteroid belt, Ceres (left), is 588 miles (946 km) in diameter—about 27% of the diameter of our moon.

Not all galaxies have rotational symmetry. Spiral galaxies are common, but there are also irregular galaxies such as the Small Magellanic Cloud. They have no organized shape and are not symmetrical.

During a solar eclipse, only a narrow band of Earth's surface will see the sun completely covered by the moon. This is called totality. Nearby areas will see the moon cover part of the sun's surface but not all of it.

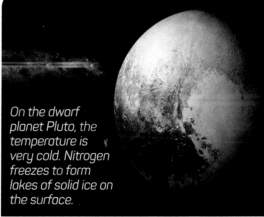

On the dwarf planet Pluto, the temperature is very cold. Nitrogen freezes to form lakes of solid ice on the surface.

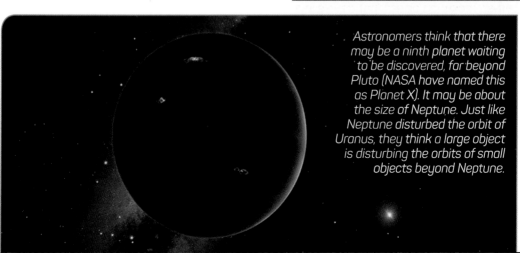

Astronomers think that there may be a ninth planet waiting to be discovered, far beyond Pluto (NASA have named this as Planet X). It may be about the size of Neptune. Just like Neptune disturbed the orbit of Uranus, they think a large object is disturbing the orbits of small objects beyond Neptune.

Index

The Author

Nancy Dickmann worked in publishing for many years before becoming a full-time author. Now, with Pushkin the Three-Legged Wonder Cat as her trusty assistant (in charge of lap-sitting), she writes books on a wide range of topics, including animals, space, history, health, and explorers. The highlight of her career so far has been getting to interview a real astronaut to find out how they use the toilet in space!